D0215591

During the Hellenistic Age, Greek scientists made important discoveries in mathematics and physics—knowledge on which many modern discoveries are based. The Greek philosopher Democritus became the first to argue that all matter was made up of invisible particles. The mathematician Euclid worked out the basic rules of geometry. Archimedes, who studied with Euclid in Alexandria, used mathematics to invent the Archimedean screw. This device, which people in Egypt still use, enabled people to raise water from the low-lying Nile to fields several feet higher.

Aristotle, Alexander's tutor

The arts also flourished in the Hellenistic world. Following the teachings of Aristotle, painters and writers created work that reflected balance and harmony. Artists strove to make accurate, three-dimensional sculptures of the human body. Writers created plays and epic poetry.

Though the Greek-speaking foreigners who settled in Egypt spread Hellenistic culture, they didn't spread their religion. Instead the foreigners adopted religious ideas from their adopted country. They were so influenced by the Egyptian religion, that the main religion in the Hellenistic Age became the worship of Egyptian divinities such as Isis. Greek-speaking artists created sculptures of the gods, and architects erected temples dedicated to different Egyptian gods, in much the same way that Egyptians had been doing for millennia.

Though the Hellenistic Age in Greece ended in the second century B.C., it continued in Egypt up to Cleopatra's day. After the Romans conquered Egypt in 30 B.C., Hellenism gradually died out there as well.

left the fields dry and parched, bringing starvation and despair.

To show their strong link to the past and to the achievements of Ptolemy and Alexander the Great, the succeeding rulers of Egypt kept the name of their dynastic founder. By tradition, every Ptolemaic king of Egypt called himself Ptolemy—and all queens were named either Arsinoë, Berenice, or Cleopatra. (Cleopatra means "glory of her father" and was the name of Alexander's sister.)

To give their dynasty the signs and symbols of legitimacy, these rulers continued Ptolemy's Egyptian-influenced religious practices. They held ceremonies where they were worshiped as ruler-gods and were depicted as Re, Isis, and Amon-Re on Egypt's imposing monuments and temples.

Ptolemy II, the son of Ptolemy I, married his sister Arsinoë II, thus beginning the custom of marrying only within the Ptolemaic family. (Since it was believed that a god could only marry another god, he and his successors married only their siblings.) Ptolemy II made Egypt the strongest country in the eastern Mediterranean. Egyptian armies marched into neighboring countries and conquered many cities. During Ptolemy II's reign, which lasted from 283 to 246 B.C., a magnificent lighthouse, Pharos, was built on the island of the same name that lay just off Alexandria's coast. Designed by the Greek architect Sostratus in 280 B.C., the Pharos symbolized the city's growing wealth and power. On top of the Pharos—which rose more than five hundred feet—burned a bright beacon of fire, visible at sea for thirty miles, to guide ships from all over the Mediterranean to the two great harbors of Alexandria.

Ptolemy III added to these achievements. He defeated several rivals of the Ptolemaic kings and conquered vast areas. By the time of Ptolemy III's rule, Alexandria had grown to be the intellectual center of the Mediterranean world, a home to brilliant scholars, engineers, mathematicians, artists, and other educated individuals. Some of the ancient world's most important inventions were conceived in this vibrant city.

After Ptolemy III's death, however, the Ptolemaic dynasty began to decline. The later Ptolemies were weak and greedy. They collected and spent vast sums of tax money to glorify themselves and their dynasty. They spent their time feasting and drinking. While they lived in luxury, the people of Alexandria and the rest of Egypt suffered through droughts and famines. The Alexandrians began to mock their kings, giving them ridiculous nicknames such as Physcon (Fatty) and Lathyrus (Chickpea).

Violent feuds and conspiracies began to occupy not only the city's life but the royal palace in Alexandria as well. The Ptolemaic dynasty did not simply pass to the eldest son or daughter. In line with Egyptian tradition, the Ptolemaic rulers elevated their favorites to the throne. In the quest to gain the king's favor and inherit the throne, the children and siblings of the Ptolemies often plotted against and even murdered one another. These feuds sometimes spread into the streets of Alexandria and to the rest of Egypt. While groups loyal to one Ptolemy or another fought bloody civil wars, the country lost most of the foreign lands it had once conquered.

At the same time, the armies of the Roman Republic, based on the Italian Peninsula, were conquering lands that had once belonged to the Ptolemies. Seeing the weak and feuding Ptolemaic kings, the Roman leaders turned their attention to the richest target in the Mediterranean world: Egypt.

In the Romans' Debt

The later Ptolemies spent enormous sums of money to build palaces and monuments, to recruit armies, and to entertain themselves. They also needed money to finance their many family feuds. In 88 B.C., to defeat his rival Ptolemy IX (Lathyrus), Ptolemy X borrowed a huge sum from a Roman moneylender. Unable to pay it back, Ptolemy X left all of Egypt to the Romans in his will. But the Romans could not collect on this promise—the will was not legal under Roman law. So the Romans allowed Lathyrus to rule over Egypt and forced the Egyptian people to pay back the personal debts of Ptolemy X.

After the death of Lathyrus in 81 B.C., Ptolemy XI came to the throne. His reign was brief. Just a few weeks after becoming king, he murdered his own step-mother and was then chased down and killed by a mob in the streets of Alexandria. His successor was Ptolemy XII (an illegitimate son of Lathyrus) who was nick-named Auletes (the Flute Player) by the Alexandrians.

Auletes had six children by two wives. With Cleopatra Tryphaena, Auletes had two daughters, Cleopatra VI (who disappeared sometime between 58 B.C. and 55 B.C.) and Berenice IV. In 69 B.C., the couple had another daughter whom they also named Cleopatra—the future Queen Cleopatra VII. Shortly after Cleopatra VII's birth, her mother died. Auletes remarried and then had two sons, Ptolemy XIII and Ptolemy XIV, and a daughter, Arsinoë IV. The members of Auletes' family would spend the rest of their lives conspiring against one another for the richest prize of all—unrivaled mastery over Egypt.

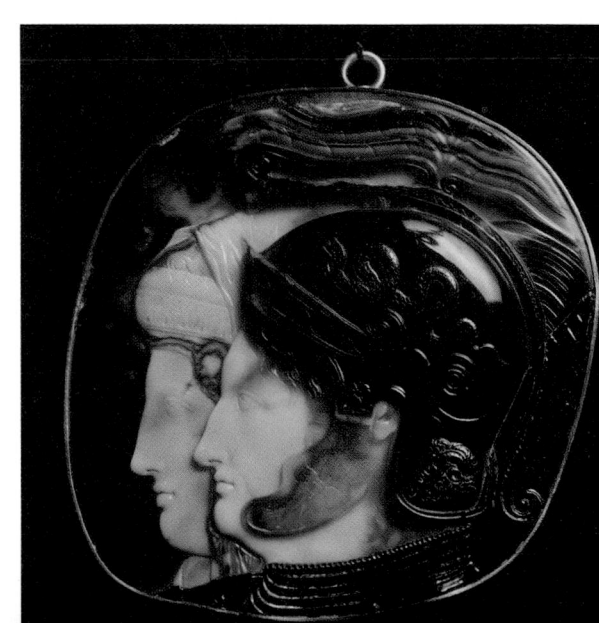

Ptolemaic rulers had their portrait carved in relief out of gems and coins. This third century B.C. portrait of Ptolemy II and his sister and wife, Arsinoë II, was carved out of sardonyx.

In the time of the Ptolemies, the Library in Alexandria housed an enormous collection of the works of ancient scholars.

Chapter **TWO**

A DANGEROUS AND VIOLENT WORLD

CLEOPATRA **VII** AND HER SIBLINGS GREW UP IN A palace complex that lay along the shores of Alexandria's eastern harbor. Marble, alabaster, and onyx columns lined the rooms of the palace. Alexandrian artists decorated these rooms with statues, busts, elaborate floor mosaics, and beautiful wall paintings. The palace had wide porches that looked out over the city, the Mediterranean Sea, and the surrounding gardens, which held beautiful fountains and iron cages where wild animals caught on the African plains were kept as pets. In the treasury room, the rulers stored a fortune in gold, precious stones, and jewelry. Cleopatra's father and his family were surrounded by hundreds of servants, the best doctors and teachers, cooks, and a small army of palace guards.

Cleopatra studied with tutors who lived in the palace with the royal family. She also attended the Museum, where she received an exceptionally good education. She learned mathematics, philosophy, literature, art, music, medicine, and foreign languages. By the time she was an adult, she could speak Egyptian, Greek, Aramaic, Hebrew, Ethiopic, and Latin, the language of the Romans.

The suspicion and scheming among Auletes' sons and daughters, however, made the luxurious palace a violent and dangerous place to live. As a young girl, Cleopatra discovered that many members of her family had been murdered by their kin. Some had been poisoned, others had been stabbed by paid assassins. She also learned that there was no law stating who would become the next king or queen. Auletes, like the Ptolemies before him, would simply choose the next ruler as he pleased from among his six descendants.

In this world, Cleopatra learned she must always stay on her guard. She must watch her brothers and sisters carefully, as they were just as ambitious as she. If she lost the contest for power, there was a good chance she would also lose her life. If she won, she would have to get rid of the others to protect herself from their scheming plots of revenge. In this life-or-death struggle, she could not trust anyone. She was always under guard and carefully followed by the soldiers and servants who were loyal to her siblings. Her scheming brothers and sisters knew of her every movement, as she knew of theirs.

Cleopatra slowly became aware that many people in Alexandria despised her father and his dynasty for their greed, corruption, and constant plotting and conspiracies. At times, even as she watched from the high porches of her palace, crowds of angry people would

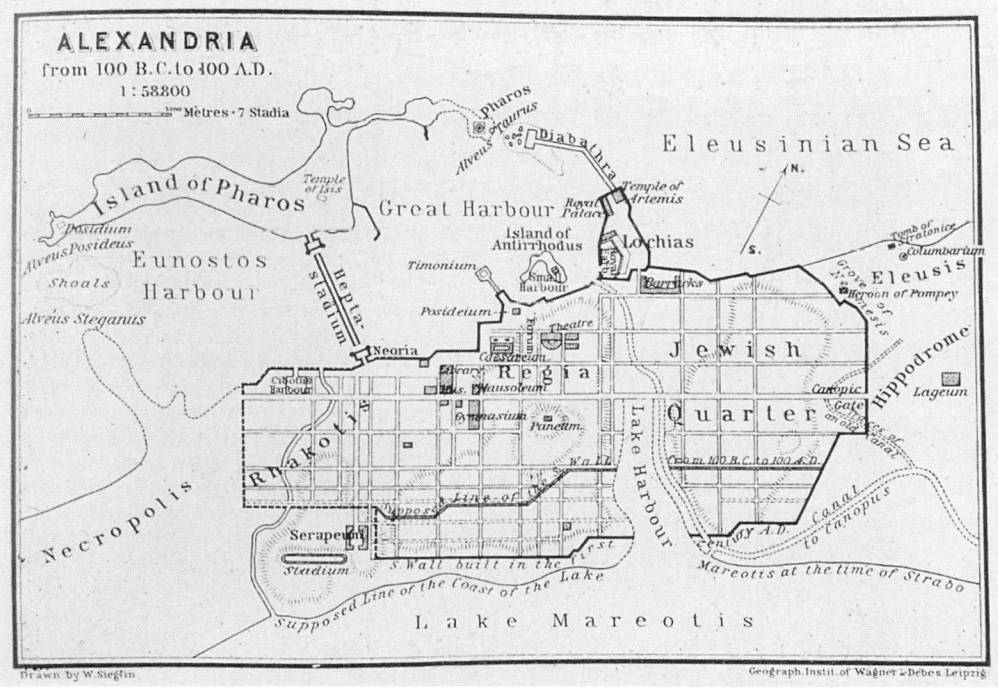

Alexandria in the time of Cleopatra

fight with soldiers and guards in the streets, causing endless trouble for their unpopular king.

In this turbulent world, one fear outweighed all others for the Ptolemies—the fear of being conquered and dominated by a foreign power. Auletes and his family knew that the Romans coveted the money and treasures of Egypt. Roman soldiers had already conquered Greece, Macedonia, parts of North Africa, and Asia Minor. Roman governors ruled these conquered lands and collected taxes from farmers, traders, and townspeople. The governors sent tributes of money and goods back to Rome and, in the meantime, built huge treasuries for themselves.

But the leaders of the Roman Republic hesitated before sending their armies into Egypt. Nearly five centuries earlier, the Romans had replaced their monarchy with a republic—a state without a king or emperor. Their republic had two consuls (heads of state) who were elected annually, senators (lawmakers) and citizens (voters). Roman leaders didn't want any single citizen to gather too much power and wealth. They knew that the man who conquered Egypt would soon become the richest and most powerful Roman of all—a king in his own right who might turn his soldiers against Rome itself.

A GANG OF THREE

By the first century B.C., the Roman Republic had changed. The consuls worked in the shadow of Rome's military commanders. These commanders fattened their own treasuries with foreign goods and land conquered by armies personally loyal to them. At times, these generals grew strong enough to seize control of the entire Roman state. In 65 B.C., the three most powerful generals—Julius Caesar, Cnaeus Pompeius Magnus (Pompey), and Marcus Licinius Crassus—set up a triumvirate (a group of three) to act as Rome's heads of state. The actions of Caesar and his partners brought the traditional Roman republic closer to becoming a dictatorship—a state under the control of a single leader.

The triumvirs, or members of the Triumvirate, realized that they must have the support of the public to maintain their power in Rome. To win that support, they put on great celebrations. Caesar, Pompey, and Crassus competed to put on the finest display of personal wealth and glory and to buy the people's loyalty with public games and feasts. They built up their own armies to conquer foreign territory, bringing new goods to the Romans. Each of the triumvirs also spent much time raising the money needed to support armies, public events, and lavish households.

In Egypt, Auletes saw that his country was growing more vulnerable to takeover by the Romans. Sooner or later, the leaders of Rome would bring their armies to the gates of Alexandria. They would conquer Egypt, seize the palace and treasury, put an end to the Ptolemaic dynasty, and impose Roman governors and Roman taxes on the Egyptians.

Auletes decided to make a deal with these Romans in order to keep his country independent. In 59 B.C., he offered a huge bribe of six thousand talents (the equivalent of many millions of dollars in modern currency) to the members of the Triumvirate. Caesar and the others gladly accepted the money, and in exchange, had the Roman Senate pass an official declaration stating that Auletes was the "friend and ally of the Roman people." Because of Auletes' bribe, Egypt could stay free of Rome—for the time being.

Auletes did not have the money on hand, however. To pay this bribe, he had to borrow funds from a Roman moneylender named Gaius Rabirius Postumus. In order to pay the money back, he would have to heavily tax his people. While Auletes kept his palace and his throne, the economy of Egypt suffered and many people starved for the sake of his corrupt dynasty.

WHEN IN ROME . . .

Auletes soon found out that his bribe did not win him much respect from the Romans. In 57 B.C., a Roman general named Cato seized the Egyptian-owned island of Cyprus. Although Cyprus was ruled by Auletes' brother, the king of Egypt did nothing to save the island. Rather than become a prisoner of the Romans, Auletes' brother committed suicide.

The people of Alexandria rebelled against Auletes for not helping his brother and for the many other humiliations Egypt was suffering. Street riots swept through the capital, reaching the walls of the Ptolemaic palace. Afraid for his life, Auletes fled the country in a ship bound for Rome. Since the Romans had declared him a "friend and ally," he believed he would be safe there and that the Romans might help him regain control of Egypt.

Auletes' daughter Berenice took this chance to proclaim herself Egypt's new ruler. Disgusted with Auletes, many Egyptian soldiers and ministers proclaimed their loyalty to her. In Rome, Auletes made another promise of an even larger bribe of ten thousand talents. The money would go to Pompey, Julius Caesar, and a Roman named Aulus Gabinius, the governor of Syria. In return, Gabinius agreed to attack Berenice and restore Auletes to the throne. Auletes left

An engraving of Berenice IV, Cleopatra's older sister

Rome to take refuge in the city of Ephesus, in Asia Minor, while awaiting his daughter's defeat.

MARCHING ON EGYPT

Gabinius declared war on Berenice and headed his Roman legions (army divisions of fifteen to twenty thousand men each) south to Egypt. In his company was the Roman moneylender Postumus, anxious to secure his share of Egypt's treasury. At the head of Gabinius's cavalry force was a twenty-five-year-old Roman officer named Mark Antony.

Gabinius and Antony conquered Pelusium, a fortified city on the eastern Egyptian border. They crossed the delta of the Nile River and arrived at Alexandria. There they defeated the Egyptians fighting under the husband of Berenice.

Terrified by the skilled Roman armies, the soldiers fighting for Berenice deserted her, and Gabinius took her prisoner. As soon as Auletes heard of his daughter's capture, he ordered her execution. Gabinius then pardoned the soldiers who had fought against Auletes and ordered a garrison of Roman soldiers to remain in Alexandria to protect him. These "Gabinians" would also ensure that Egypt would repay the vast sums Auletes had promised Gabinius and his Roman allies. Roman cargo ships were soon docking at Alexandria to transport cargoes of grain and chests of money back to Rome.

Just a few years later, in 51 B.C., Auletes died. In the

meantime, he had given much thought to his successor. He realized that Cleopatra had the intelligence and skill to rule in his place and to keep the Romans at bay. But in ancient Egypt, a queen could not rule alone—she had to have a king. So Auletes decided that eighteen-year-old Cleopatra would rule the country jointly with her younger half brother, ten-year-old Ptolemy XIII.

Cleopatra portrayed on a gold coin, 36 B.C.

Chapter **THREE**

SISTER AND BROTHER

IN MANY WAYS, CLEOPATRA IS STILL A MYSTERY. Historians know about her actions and her reputation only through the writings of ancient Greeks and Romans. Nobody recorded Cleopatra's own words or wrote down her opinions. Even her appearance is still a mystery. Small, timeworn coins made in Alexandria from Cleopatra's time show only her profile, with a strong chin, heavy brows, and a large hooked nose. A few busts of Egyptian women found in the Middle East come from Cleopatra's time. They may represent her, but nobody knows for sure.

Several ancient historians wrote descriptions of Cleopatra. Most of them lived after Cleopatra's time, however, and could only write down what others had told them about her. Plutarch heard descriptions of Cleopatra passed down from members of his family who had served as the queen's doctors. In one of his books, he reported:

> Her actual beauty... was not in itself so remarkable that none could be compared with her, or that no one could see her without being struck by it, but the contact of her presence, if you lived with her, was irresistible; the attraction of her person, joining with the charm of her conversation, and the character that attended all she said or did, was something bewitching. It was a pleasure merely to hear the sound of her voice, with which, like an instrument of many strings, she could pass from one language to another.

As charming and intelligent as she was, Cleopatra still had to share power with her ten-year-old half brother, Ptolemy XIII. Though this brother was still too young to match wits with Cleopatra, he had three loyal, ambitious, and scheming advisers: Pothinus, Achillas, and Theodotus. These men worked to get Cleopatra off the throne—hoping even to kill her—and thus help Ptolemy become sole ruler of Egypt.

Pothinus managed the servants and guards of the royal palace. Achillas commanded the Egyptian army, one of the largest and most powerful in the world. Theodotus, a teacher of rhetoric (public speaking), was

CLEOPATRA AS ISIS

A s queen, Cleopatra continued the Egyptian tradition of ruler-divinity. She identified herself as Isis, the goddess who was considered by the Egyptians to be the mother of humankind and who made the Nile rise each year, making the land fruitful. Cleopatra commissioned sculptors to carve her as Isis, and metalsmiths to cast coins showing her as the goddess. When she appeared in public, the royal crown she wore showed snakes symbolizing Re and a crescent moon symbolizing Isis.

This statuette of Isis and her son Horus was made centuries before Cleopatra's time.

Ptolemy's tutor. He advised the young king on how to deal with the Romans and with his older sister.

Cleopatra decided it was essential that she make herself known to the Egyptians. She wanted to show that she would carry on and honor their traditions. In March of 51 B.C., just after becoming queen, she traveled up the Nile to the city of Thebes. There she took part in a ceremony dedicated to the god Amon-Re. The modern historian Michael Foss wrote of this visit:

> She was not just a Macedonian Greek from Alexandria who farmed an alien land for her own benefit from the distant Mediterranean shore. She was an Egyptian whose heart beat in time with the pharaonic tradition, a queen of all her people.

This trip did not boost Cleopatra's popularity with the Egyptians as much as she had hoped. Cleopatra and her half brother had come to power during a national crisis. The spring floods of the Nile had not been abundant and the harvests were poor. The people were suffering under a famine. They grew restless and rebellious. Pothinus spread propaganda against Cleopatra that made the people even angrier toward her.

By 48 B.C., Cleopatra felt herself to be in serious danger from Ptolemy's advisers. She fled Alexandria and traveled to Syria, where she built up a small army and waited for a chance to return.

Meanwhile, Rome's ruling Triumvirate came to an end when Crassus died fighting in Parthia (the empire that has since become Iran and Iraq). This left Pompey and Caesar—who then turned against each other and began fighting a civil war. In 48 B.C., Caesar defeated Pompey at Pharsalia in Greece, thus becoming the most powerful leader in Rome.

The fifty-four-year-old Caesar was ambitious, ruthless, and brilliant as a military commander. He was most admired for his courage in battle and for his generosity to his soldiers. Plutarch, the Greek historian, wrote:

[Caesar] was so much master of the goodwill and service of his soldiers that those who in other expeditions were but ordinary men displayed a courage past defeating or withstanding when they went upon any danger where Caesar's glory was concerned. . . . [T]here was no danger to which he did not willingly expose himself, no labor from which he pleaded an exemption. His contempt of danger was not so much wondered at by his soldiers because they knew how much he coveted honor. But his enduring so much hardship, which he did to all appearance beyond his natural strength, very much astonished them. For he was a spare man, had a soft and white skin. . . . [B]y indefatigable journeys, coarse diet, frequent lodging in the field, and continual laborious exercise, he . . . fortified his body against all attacks.

The beaten Pompey sailed with his army southward, across the Mediterranean Sea to Egypt. He was looking for help, in the form of money and food, from young Ptolemy XIII. Pompey planned to enlist the Gabinian soldiers (the Roman soldiers who had traveled to Alexandria to overthrow Berenice), who were still living in Egypt. But Achillas, Pothinus, and Theodotus had different plans. Seeing Caesar as the winner in the civil war and Pompey as the loser, they plotted to murder Pompey as soon as he arrived in Egypt. They believed Caesar would be grateful and would show his gratitude by helping them to get rid of Cleopatra.

When Pompey and his small fleet arrived at the Egyptian coast, Ptolemy's military commander and a few soldiers rowed a small boat out to Pompey's ship. Though Pompey's wife sensed something was wrong and warned him not to go aboard, he climbed in. As the boat was rowed toward shore, a Roman soldier loyal to Ptolemy stabbed Pompey in the back. As Pompey's wife screamed in horror, the body was rowed ashore, where Pompey's head was cut off. Theodotus kept the head to present as a token of friendship to Julius Caesar.

FIGHTING FOR ALEXANDRIA

During this same time, Julius Caesar had been chasing Pompey from Greece to Egypt. He was worried that Pompey would rally a fresh army in Egypt.

One of the greatest military leaders of all time, Julius Caesar was also an accomplished politician, writer, and public speaker.

Caesar intended to capture Alexandria and defeat Pompey once and for all while he still had the advantage. In need of money for his campaigns, Caesar also intended to personally collect the long-overdue debts owed by the late Auletes.

After a four-day voyage, Caesar landed in Egypt with ten ships and four thousand soldiers. When he arrived at the palace complex in Alexandria, Theodotus greeted him with the head of Pompey. But instead of congratulating Theodotus for this cold-blooded murder, Caesar dismissed him with scorn. Caesar had been Pompey's enemy, but the miserable death that Pompey had suffered—being treacherously stabbed in the back instead of honorably defeated on the field of battle—angered Caesar.

Pothinus, Achillas, and Theodotus waited anxiously for the victorious Caesar to leave Egypt. But instead of returning to Rome, Caesar decided to remain in the palace complex in Alexandria. He would collect the money that Egypt still owed to Rome by raiding Egypt's treasury. To persuade Pompey's soldiers to come over to his side, Caeser granted them a pardon for fighting against him in the civil war.

Caesar decided to use his influence to end the feud between Ptolemy and Cleopatra. He wanted the two siblings to rule Egypt together, as their father had wished. In so doing, Caesar believed he would make himself and Rome even stronger. He would allow the siblings to rule, while enriching himself and Rome by collecting taxes and tributes from the Egyptians. Best of all, he would do all this without having to fight a single battle.

Ptolemy's three advisers weren't interested, however. If Caesar and Rome were in control of Alexandria, their own power would decline. So they plotted to get Caesar and his army out of Alexandria. Achillas made life difficult for the Romans by ordering moldy grain to be delivered to the Roman soldiers. He also stirred up an anti-Roman rebellion among the citizens of Alexandria. Street battles broke out between the citizens and Roman soldiers, and many people on both sides were killed. Meanwhile, Achillas's army returned to Alexandria from Pelusium, where it had been watching for Cleopatra's return to Egypt.

SNEAKING IN

To reunite the feuding siblings, Caesar summoned Ptolemy and Cleopatra to the palace. But Cleopatra would have to pass Achillas's army to reach the palace grounds. She knew that if Achillas's men captured her, they would probably murder her.

According to legend, Cleopatra came up with a daring plan to sneak into Alexandria. She approached the enemy lines, then set off in a small boat with a merchant, Apollodorus of Sicily, a friend and ally. After reaching Alexandria, Cleopatra and Apollodorus sailed into the small harbor near the palace. Apollodorus then wrapped Cleopatra in a carpet.

Roman soldiers and Egyptian guards closely watched the halls and doors of the palace. Apollodorus, dressed as a servant, passed the guards with the heavy bundle thrown over his shoulder. In this way he was able to bring Cleopatra safely into the chambers occupied by Caesar. There, while Caesar and his many guards watched, Apollodorus unrolled the carpet, and the queen of Egypt tumbled out before the leader of Rome.

Cleopatra was only twenty-one years old, but her boldness and cleverness fascinated Caesar. Her intelligence and her royal ancestry were far more interesting than mere beauty to the Roman leader, who was thirty-one years older than she. Within just a few days, or perhaps even that same night, Caesar and Cleopatra became lovers.

A Turn for the Worse

Caesar ordered Ptolemy to reconcile with his sister. He asked the two siblings to rule Egypt jointly, as Auletes had decreed in his will. Cleopatra agreed, as she knew Caesar supported her. On the advice of

According to legend, Julius Caesar was pleasantly surprised when the twenty-one-year-old Cleopatra rolled out of a carpet to greet him.

Pothinus, Ptolemy also agreed, but only as a way to buy time. Keenly aware of Caesar's allegiance to Cleopatra, Ptolemy would wait until the Roman general left Egypt before trying once again to grab power for himself.

Cleopatra watched and waited. She knew that she would never be able to rule peacefully with her half brother, whose advisers were determined to get rid of her. Pothinus had turned most of the Alexandrians and the people of Egypt against her, and Achillas controlled the Egyptian army. Cleopatra could do nothing until Caesar defeated Ptolemy and his advisers.

Achillas realized that Caesar backed Cleopatra in this struggle, and that Caesar would not leave unless he were defeated and driven back to Rome. Later that year, from his camp outside Alexandria, Achillas commanded twenty thousand men to march on Alexandria. The army occupied the city and surrounded the palace. Seeing Caesar caught in a trap, the people of Alexandria began rioting against the Roman soldiers. Inside the palace, the Roman guards closely watched Cleopatra, Ptolemy, Pothinus, and Arsinoë, Cleopatra's younger half sister. As long as Caesar's army held out, none of the royal family would be harmed. But Caesar would allow none of them to leave.

The standoff continued. Convinced that Caesar would lose in the coming war, Arsinoë slipped out of the palace, joined Achillas in the camps, and proclaimed herself the new queen of Egypt and coruler with

Ptolemy XIII. Pothinus and Ptolemy made plans to join Arsinoë, but word of the plan soon leaked to Caesar. Suspecting that Pothinus was planning to kill him, Caesar ordered his Roman guards to arrest Pothinus and put him to death for treason.

QUEEN OF EGYPT

Caesar's guards controlled the inside of the palace while his troops fought in the city streets with Achillas's men. Caesar himself led the fight both on land and in the harbor. While battles raged between Roman and Egyptian galleys (battleships rowed by slaves), Cleopatra watched from the windows and porches of the palace.

In the meantime, Cleopatra's enemies clashed in the Egyptian camps outside Alexandria. Arsinoë and her adviser Ganymedes quarreled bitterly with Achillas. Soon thereafter, Ganymedes arranged for his guards to murder Achillas. After Achillas was murdered, Ganymedes took control of the army, continuing the attack on the palace and on the Roman ships.

Caesar searched for a way to defeat the Egyptian army. Cleopatra may have given him the idea to allow Ptolemy to leave the palace. Cleopatra and Caesar knew that Ptolemy would join Arsinoë and Ganymedes. If the three of them quarreled, as Ganymedes had quarreled with Achillas, their army would be vulnerable to a surprise attack.

In the meantime, Roman reinforcements began

arriving in Egypt from Syria. These troops attacked the Egyptians from the east. On March 27 of 47 B.C., Caesar took the offensive. He marched out of Alexandria to battle the Egyptians along the shores of Lake Mareotis. The Roman soldiers were outnumbered, but they fought with more discipline than the Egyptians. They easily defeated the Egyptian troops, many of whom deserted Ptolemy and ran for their lives. As the Roman troops massacred enemy survivors, fourteen-year-old Ptolemy XIII drowned in the Nile River while fleeing in his heavy, gold-plated armor. Soon after the battle, Caesar's troops captured Arsinoë and took her prisoner.

Caesar had become the master of Egypt, but direct rule over Egypt did not interest him. He trusted Cleopatra to rule Egypt as his ally. At twenty-two years of age, she was an energetic and intelligent woman, and she had Caesar's full support.

According to ancient Egyptian custom, however, a queen needed a king. At Caesar's direction, Cleopatra formally married her younger half brother, Ptolemy XIV. Cleopatra made sure that this Ptolemy had no scheming advisers such as Pothinus or Achillas to help him contest Cleopatra's rule. Only twelve years old, Ptolemy XIV was too young to effectively share power or fight his older half sister.

Some historians believe this ancient bust is of Cleopatra.

Chapter **FOUR**

CLEOPATRA AND CAESAR

INSTEAD OF RETURNING IMMEDIATELY TO ROME, Caesar remained in Egypt to enjoy a few months of relaxation. Determined to amuse Caesar and to solidify his alliance with her, Cleopatra ordered her servants to prepare her royal barge for a voyage that would take the lovers up the Nile. According to some ancient historians, the ship was three hundred feet long and decorated with marble and gold. It held beautiful banquet halls, stately rooms, and lush gardens.

With some of Caesar's army sailing alongside, Cleopatra's barge made its way up the Nile, stopping at cities and temples along the river. Cleopatra proudly stood at Caesar's side, appearing before her subjects to demonstrate her role as queen, principal ruler, and friend and ally of Rome's strongest leader. She was also pregnant with Caesar's child, a son who would be born on June 23, 47 B.C.

Caesar and Cleopatra may have been in love, but they were also practical and shrewd. Each found the other a useful partner in their common goal of winning further glory and power. Cleopatra needed Rome's protection, and Caesar needed the prestige of having influence over Egypt and its wealth. Cleopatra and Caesar may even have been planning to start an entirely new dynasty that would combine the Ptolemies with Caesar's Roman family. Joined together, Egypt and Rome would form a domain even larger than the one Alexander had conquered. Cleopatra believed her child, Caesarion, would inherit Egypt and rule as the first king of this new empire in Alexandria. The capital city of Egypt would be transformed into the capital of the world.

THE TRIUMPHS OF CAESAR

After the romantic Nile River voyage, Caesar could no longer ignore the urgent messages calling him to return to Rome. Following a sad farewell, Caesar sailed home. He left behind three legions to keep order in Alexandria and to support Cleopatra, if necessary, against rivals within Egypt or enemies outside her borders.

In September of 46 B.C., Caesar celebrated his latest military victories with grand military parades (called

A stone relief of Cleopatra, left, *with her son,* right. *Realizing that Caesar was the father, the Alexandrians nicknamed the child Caesarion, or Little Caesar.*

triumphs) through the Roman Forum, the central public square of the city and center of government. While Caesar's legions marched in these triumphs, the Romans stood along the streets to hail the victor and to see his prisoners walking behind him in chains. The most elaborate of Caesar's triumphs celebrated his victory against the Egyptians.

Shuffling along in chains at the head of the prisoners was Cleopatra's half-sister Arsinoë. Triumphs were a Roman tradition, and by custom the prisoners were executed after the ceremonies. But the humiliation of the young Egyptian princess angered some Roman citizens. For this reason, Caesar decided to spare Arsinoë's life.

Soon after the triumph, Caesar invited Cleopatra to visit Rome as an independent ruler and ally. Cleopatra sailed to Rome with Caesarion. She also took young Ptolemy XIV to keep him from rallying against her while she was gone. She moved into Caesar's palace on the west bank of the Tiber River, which flows through the center of Rome.

To honor Cleopatra, Caesar built a new temple dedicated to the Roman goddess Venus. Next to Venus, he put up a statue of Cleopatra as the Egyptian goddess Isis, following the Egyptian custom of portraying rulers as divine beings. It was the first time in Roman history that a human being was represented in public as a god. Caesar's actions surprised and angered the Romans, who suspected Cleopatra of using Caesar in the service of her own ambitions.

THE ROYAL FAMILY

To the people of Rome, Cleopatra was no goddess. She was a foreigner, an Egyptian descended from Macedonians. Worse, she was a woman who held absolute, royal power—something unheard of in Rome's history. The Romans would allow Caesar a love affair with such a woman—after all, he had defeated the Egyptian army and could do whatever he liked with what they saw to be the "spoils" of this victory. But they believed that inviting a foreign queen to live with him in Rome and raising a statue to her in the center of the city was going too far.

ANCIENT CALENDARS

Rome gained a new calendar because of Caesar's liaison with Cleopatra. The Romans counted 355 days in their year, with an extra month added every other year. The Senate had to officially declare this extra month—an action the senators did not always bother to take. Because the extra month was not always added, after a few years, the Roman calendar did not match the seasons. By Caesar's lifetime, the calendar was about three months ahead! While Caesar was in Egypt, Cleopatra introduced Caesar to the Greek astronomer Sosigenes, who offered Caesar a solution to the problem of the ever-changing Roman calendar.

For over two thousand years, the Egyptians had been using a calendar cycle that was more accurate than the Roman calendar. The Egyptian calendar was based on the sun's 365-day cycle. Sosigenes suggested that the Romans adopt a new calendar of 365 days, with twelve months per year and an extra day (a "leap day") in February of every fourth year. Caesar agreed to the idea. To allow the seasons to catch up with the new calendar, the year 46 B.C. was officially extended to 445 days. The next year, 45 B.C., Rome adopted the Julian calendar—which was in effect for more than fifteen hundred years.

By the sixteenth century A.D., however, the Julian calendar was ten days behind the dates on which the seasons had actually begun. In A.D. 1582, Pope Gregory XIII corrected the Julian calendar by ordering that ten days be dropped from that year. To permanently correct the Julian calendar, he decreed that February would still have an extra day every fourth year—with the exception of century years (the individual years that mark a new century, such as 1600, 1700, and 1800). An extra day would be added only to century years that are divisible by four hundred (such as 1600 and 2000) and not in century years that are not divisible by four hundred (such as 1700 and 1900). This Gregorian calendar is what we use today in the Western world.

Caesar's actions particularly angered Rome's patricians (upper-class members of Roman society). He made no secret about keeping an Egyptian mistress while remaining married to a Roman named Calpurnia. Furthermore, Caesar, Cleopatra, and Caesarion appeared to many Romans as a royal family. The patricians felt that Caesar threatened them with a return to hereditary monarchy, the type of government the Romans had overthrown hundreds of years earlier and replaced with a republic.

Roman soldiers and common citizens still felt a strong loyalty to Caesar, however. He had fought and won many battles and had captured immense territories in Europe and Asia. Shortly after the triumphs of Caesar, the Senate had appointed him the sole consul of Rome for five years. Caesar used his power to expel members of the Senate who opposed him and then replaced them with his friends. At Cleopatra's urging, he had the Senate officially declare Cleopatra and Ptolemy to be the "Friends and Allies of Rome." He also ordered an official named Cinna to prepare a decree allowing him to marry Cleopatra and as many other women as he wished.

Slowly but surely, Caesar was turning the Roman republic into an empire, with himself as emperor. What would Caesar do, some Romans wondered, if he remained under what they considered to be Cleopatra's spell? The patricians were terrified he would declare himself king—a word hated by every Roman.

PAYING NO HEED

Still feeling restless, Caesar sought new enemies to conquer on the battlefield. In the spring of 45 B.C., he defeated Pompey's sons at Munda, in what has since become Spain. In early 44 B.C., he prepared for a campaign against Parthia. Parthia had been an unconquerable land up to that point—though many men had tried. Among the Romans, as Caesar knew, anyone who could defeat the fierce Parthians would be considered a military leader as fine as Alexander the Great. Caesar planned to leave Rome around the Ides (or middle day) of March. Cleopatra did not want to remain in the city without him—she had many enemies among the patricians and among Caesar's other rivals. She made plans to leave Rome and return to Egypt.

At the same time, several leading Romans, led by two men named Brutus and Cassius, were devising a

Alexander the Great, the fourth century B.C. founder of Alexandria

plot to assassinate Caesar. The conspirators believed that Caesar would soon proclaim himself king. They believed that Rome's commoners wanted to bring back the republic that Caesar's rule was on the verge of ending.

Rumors of the conspiracy swirled around the streets and public squares of Rome. Friends warned Caesar, but he ignored them. He had faced many dangerous enemies and plots against his life and had prevailed. In

The death of Julius Caesar painted in 1793 by Italian artist Vincenzo Camuccini

Rome, where the general population seemed to adore him and support his every action, he felt confident.

On the Ides of March, 44 B.C., Brutus and Cassius gathered with a group of more than twenty Roman senators in the Senate hall. Shortly after Caesar entered the hall, the conspirators crowded around him, holding daggers under their cloaks. At a signal, they ran forward, stabbing Caesar in a frenzy while he desperately fought them off. None of the Roman senators watching the attack acted to protect him. Within minutes, Caesar lay dead at the foot of the statue of his old enemy Pompey.

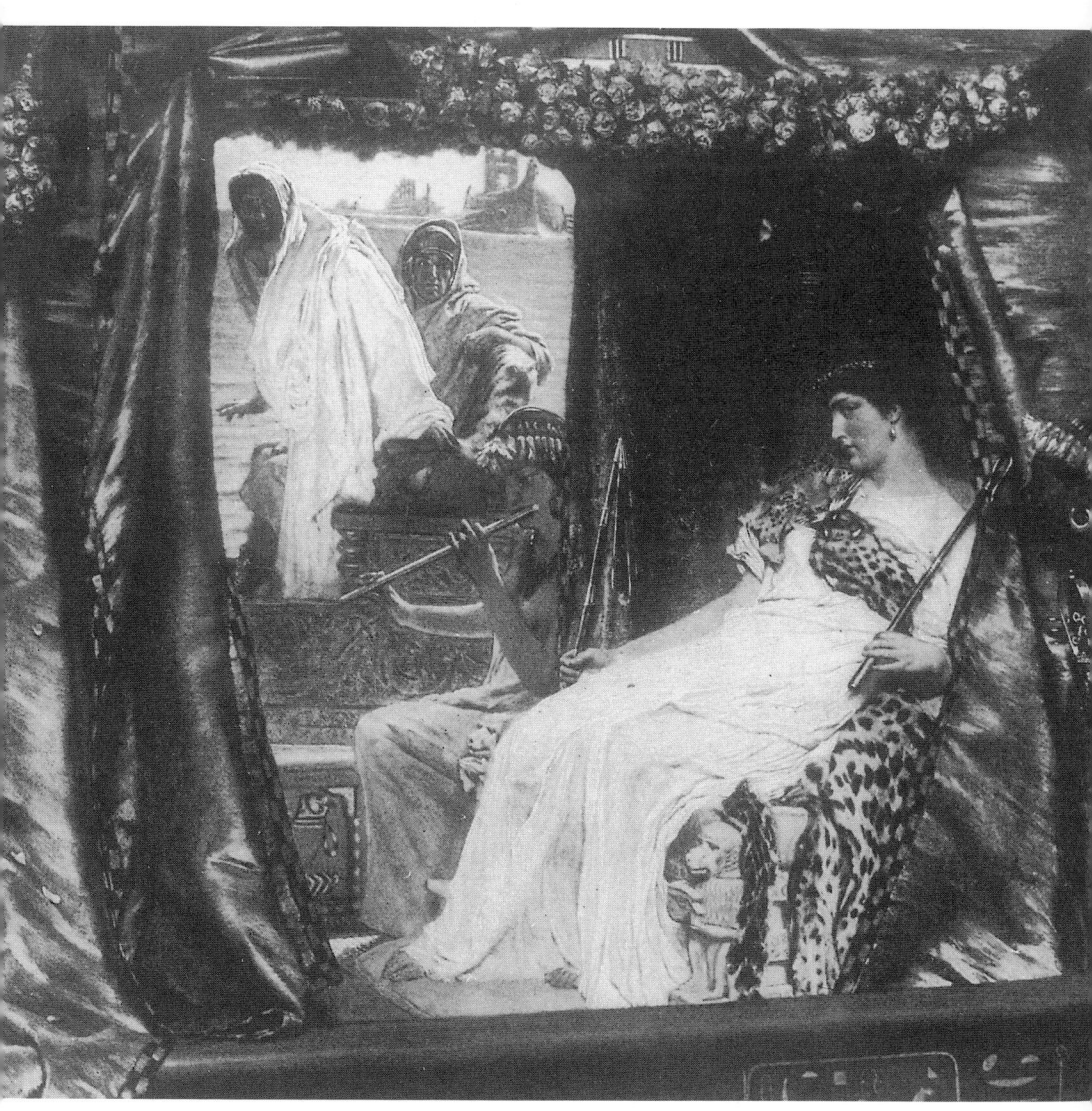

Mark Antony gazes at Cleopatra aboard her majestic royal barge.

Chapter **FIVE**

CLEOPATRA AND ANTONY

WITH CAESAR DEAD, HIS ASSASSINS BEGAN BATTLING his allies in the streets of Rome. Brutus and Cassius soon discovered they had been wrong about what the common citizens wanted. Among the people, Caesar remained a hero—and had become a martyr. While mobs rioted, hunting down and murdering many of the conspirators, Brutus and Cassius fled Rome.

At Caesar's palace on the hills overlooking the Tiber, a messenger brought Cleopatra the news of Caesar's assassination. Cleopatra and Caesarion were now alone in a foreign city, far from their home and— Cleopatra believed—in great danger from Caesar's enemies. She rushed to Ostia, the port of Rome, and sailed back home in the ship that had brought her to

Rome two years earlier. Shortly after she arrived in Alexandria, Ptolemy XIV, the last sibling to share power with her, was murdered—perhaps on Cleopatra's orders. Cleopatra then proclaimed her son Caesarion as Ptolemy XV Caesar, her new coruler. She believed that placing her half Roman son at her side would strengthen her ties to the future leader of Rome, whoever he might be.

In the meantime, Mark Antony, Caesar's friend and comrade during many of his campaigns, had given a moving speech at Caesar's funeral in the Roman Forum. As William Shakespeare would write centuries later in his play *Antony and Cleopatra*, Antony declared:

> You all did love him once, not without cause:
> What cause witholds you, then, to mourn for him?
> O judgment, thou art fled to brutish beasts,
> And men have lost their reason—Bear with me;
> My heart is in the coffin there with Caesar,
> And I must pause till it come back to me.

The Roman crowds greatly admired Antony's speech, which nobly expressed the sadness that many of them were feeling. In a frenzy of outrage and grief, the Romans built an immense funeral pyre for Caesar in the Roman Forum. Presiding over the ceremony was the great nephew of Julius Caeser, Gaius Octavius—a young man who was preparing himself to succeed Julius Caesar as Rome's leader.

Mark Antony addresses the Romans over the body of Julius Caesar.

In 43 B.C., Antony allied with Octavius and Marcus Aemilius Lepidus, the least powerful of the three. In his will, Caesar had named the nineteen-year-old Octavius his adopted son and heir. (Caesar had not mentioned Cleopatra or Caesarion in his will—by Roman law, foreigners could not inherit Roman property.) Antony, Octavius, and Lepidus agreed to form the second Triumvirate.

CHOOSING SIDES

The triumvirs then drew up long lists of their enemies. They accused several thousand people of being part of the conspiracy against Caesar. On the triumvirs' orders, the lands and money of the accused were taken away and hundreds were murdered. With the money taken from the accused, Antony raised an army to fight Brutus and Cassius, who had sailed across the Adriatic Sea to Greece. Both sides in this new civil war needed ships and soldiers, and both sides were seeking help from Cleopatra.

Cleopatra realized that she must choose very carefully. If she helped the winner of this war, she and Caesarion would remain in control of Egypt. If she sent help to the side that lost, the winners would take vengeance on her by conquering Egypt and appointing a Roman governor to replace her.

Cleopatra decided to side with the Triumvirate against Brutus and Cassius. The triumvirs had won her friendship by officially recognizing Caesarion as her coruler. Cleopatra prepared the Egyptian army to sail overseas. She also sent Caesar's Roman soldiers in Egypt to march against Cassius in Syria. To Cassius himself, Cleopatra sent the message that a terrible famine was raging through Egypt, making it impossible for her to send aid.

Angry and determined to punish the queen, Cassius ordered his soldiers to march south and invade Egypt. But very soon, Brutus sent Cassius an urgent message: the triumvirs were crossing the Adriatic Sea toward Greece. Brutus and Cassius then marched onto the plains of Macedonia, where they prepared for battle against Antony, Octavius, and Lepidus.

Realizing that a battle would soon take place,

Cleopatra prepared a fleet of Egyptian warships in the harbor of Alexandria. Riding in the flagship, Cleopatra ordered the fleet to sail toward Greece. But just a few days out of harbor, the fleet ran into a heavy storm. Several Egyptian ships were lost, and Cleopatra fell ill. She ordered her ships to return to Alexandria.

In October of 42 B.C., at Philippi, Greece, the triumvirs defeated Cassius and Brutus, who both then committed suicide. The victors celebrated their triumph by dividing Rome's territory among them. Octavius would rule the West (Rome and the western Mediterranean); Antony would rule Greece and the wealthy East (territories that included Asia Minor and Syria); Lepidus would have the Roman provinces of North Africa.

To most Romans, Antony appeared to be the true heir of Julius Caesar. Antony's armies were large, he was mature and strong, he had the loyalty of the Romans, and he was an experienced military commander. Octavius, on the other hand, was still a young man. He had spent most of his life studying in Apollonia, a small Greek town on the Adriatic Sea, and had no experience of war or government leadership. Yet Julius Caesar himself had known and trusted Octavius enough to name him as his heir. Despite the fact that Octavius had no experience leading soldiers or citizens, Caesar had recognized that the young man was clever enough to handle his enemies and to master the dangerous politics of Rome.

Cleopatra soon heard of the victory of the triumvirs at Philippi. She had met Antony once before, when he helped Gabinius defeat Cleopatra's sister Berenice. This time, as queen, she saw that Antony was the strongest man in Rome, stronger than Octavius or Lepidus. Someday, she believed, the Triumvirate would end, probably in battle, and Antony would inherit Caesar's short-lived place as Rome's sole leader.

THE NEW DIONYSUS

Mark Antony had enjoyed an extravagant youth. Once, it was said, he had arranged a lavish banquet on the banks of a river, making his entrance in a chariot drawn by lions. A charismatic and outgoing man, he had spent many nights drinking and carousing in the streets of Rome. He cavorted with dancers, actors, and musicians, causing scandals and outraging the patricians. Antony was less sophisticated than Caesar and preferred physical over intellectual recreations. But after a time, Mark Antony settled down to become one of the most popular leaders in the Roman armies. Plutarch described him:

> He had a very good and noble appearance; his beard was well grown, his forehead large, and his nose aquiline, giving him altogether a bold masculine look that reminded people of the faces of Hercules in paintings and sculptures. . . . What might seem to some very insupportable, his

vaunting, his raillery, his drinking in public, sitting down by the men as they were taking their food, and eating, as he stood, at the common soldiers' tables, made him the delight and pleasure of the army. . . . And his generous ways, his open and lavish hand at gifts and favours to his friends and fellow-soldiers, did a great deal for him in his first advance to power, and after he had become great, long maintained his fortunes, when a thousand follies were hastening their overthrow.

Antony journeyed eastward to the territories he was to rule. His armies marched through Greece and Asia Minor, where the crowds hailed him as the new "emperor of the East" and worshiped him as a ruler-god. Celebrations were staged in Antony's honor, and statues appeared showing him as a god, the "New Dionysus." Dionysus was a god of wine and revels, the most popular god in the eastern Mediterranean world at that time. The followers of this god held secret rites in secluded forests, dancing, singing, and drinking themselves into a frenzy. Posing as the New Dionysus to win prestige and authority over the people, Antony gathered a court of musicians and entertainers to provide grand spectacles in the cities he now ruled. To pay for his celebrations, as well as his army, he levied heavy taxes on Rome's eastern provinces.

Antony had not yet finished conquering new lands. He was preparing to take up Caesar's battle against

Parthia. The defeat of Parthia would revenge Crassus, the triumvir who had been killed by the Parthians nine years before. Parthia's defeat would also subdue the last major kingdom in the known world to resist Roman dominance. Antony wanted to show everyone that he, rather than Octavius, was the worthy successor to Julius Caesar.

MEETING AT TARSUS

In 41 B.C., Antony reached Tarsus. He summoned Cleopatra in order to hear her explain away a rumor that she had secretly helped Cassius in the civil war. Antony also wanted her to promise support to his Parthian campaign.

Determined to impress Antony with her wealth and glamour, the queen arrived aboard the lavish barge later made famous by Plutarch in his writings. She then summoned Antony to the riverside to meet her. After some hesitation, Antony agreed to appear as Cleopatra's guest. Aboard the barge, he was treated to a dazzling sight the likes of which he had never experienced in Rome or in any foreign land. "He found the preparations to receive him magnificent beyond expression," wrote Plutarch. "The whole thing was a spectacle that has seldom been equaled for beauty." Dressed as Aphrodite, the Greek goddess of love and beauty, Cleopatra presented a fabulous banquet for Antony and his soldiers. The next night, Antony returned the favor, holding a banquet for the queen.

STRIKING BARGAINS

Cleopatra had a good understanding of men, and of Roman men in particular. She saw that Mark Antony could be just as useful to her as Julius Caesar had been. Antony commanded the largest and most experienced army in Rome. He also had the support of Rome's common people and its patricians. Even better, Antony held sway over the eastern half of Rome's territories. It was there that Cleopatra wanted to build her empire, hand in hand with Antony. Next to him, Octavius looked like an inexperienced boy.

Instantly fascinated by one another, Cleopatra and Mark Antony became lovers. Antony returned with Cleopatra to Alexandria. He was charmed by Cleopatra and intrigued by her lavish lifestyle. She, in turn, must have been attracted to his strength, courage, and good humor. Together they held extravagant parties in the palace and frolicked in the streets of Alexandria. According to some accounts, they disguised themselves as servants to roam the city and play pranks on the people they met.

The lovers also struck a political deal. Antony needed Cleopatra's help in his campaign to attack Parthia. Cleopatra promised to support Antony by supplying soldiers and money to the legions that Antony was gathering. In return, Antony promised to order the murder of Arsinoë, who had taken refuge in the city of Ephesus, in Asia Minor. Soon Arsinoë—Cleopatra's only living sibling—was dead.

After spending the winter in Alexandria, Antony returned to Rome to settle conflicts with other members of the Triumvirate. In October, 40 B.C., he made another treaty with Octavius in Brundisium, a port city southeast of Rome. The two men would retain the division between eastern and western Rome. They would also allow Lepidus, the weakest triumvir, to continue governing the less wealthy northern Africa territories. To seal the peace pact with Octavius, Antony married Octavius's beautiful and kind sister, Octavia. In Rome, marriages were often used to show goodwill and to complete a peace pact.

Displeased and hurt by the news of this marriage, the twenty-nine-year-old Cleopatra turned to her own

Sculpture of Octavia, Octavian's sister and Mark Antony's wife

affairs in Egypt. Allying herself to Antony assured her that Egypt would stay free of Roman interference, for the time being. She also held a strong claim on Antony's allegiance in the future, for that year she gave birth to Antony's twins, whom she named Alexander Helios and Cleopatra Selene. Cleopatra saw her children by Caesar and Antony as heirs to the Roman-Egyptian dynasty that she still hoped to start in Alexandria.

Soon after Antony returned to Rome, Herod—a young leader of Judaea (a small country covering part of what has since become Israel)—arrived in Alexandria seeking Cleopatra's help. Herod had been driven out of his small country by the Parthians. Knowing Cleopatra's connection to Antony, he asked for her assistance in persuading Antony to overtake the Parthians. Cleopatra gave Herod a ship to sail, as he requested. Antony helped Herod reconquer Judaea and become king, since Rome would have ultimate authority over the country.

THE RULER CLEOPATRA

For the next three and a half years, Cleopatra ably ruled her kingdom alone. Despite famine and drought, the Egyptian economy revived. Peace allowed the traders of Alexandria to carry on business without trouble. The treasury recovered from the payment of the heavy ransoms Cleopatra's father had promised the Romans.

Cleopatra knew that her father's carelessness had nearly ruined Egypt. She carefully managed Egypt's finances. Determined to increase the production of grain, Cleopatra lowered taxes on farmers.

Cleopatra took care to observe traditional religious rites, identifying herself in statues and inscriptions as Isis. She supported religious temples through allowances of food and money. And for the first time, a Ptolemaic ruler was able to speak and write in the native language of Egypt rather than in Greek. The people admired Cleopatra for her skillful diplomacy and her determination to resist annexation by Rome.

Cleopatra reigned alone and unopposed; the uprisings common in Auletes' time had stopped. Her sibling rivals had died in battle or had been executed. The army remained loyal to the queen, and since she also had Antony's support, no foreigner dared to attack her. Her children, meanwhile, were prepared by tutors and advisers for the responsibilities that awaited them.

UNEASY ALLIANCES

In 37 B.C., Antony and Octavius made another agreement to continue the Triumvirate, this time at the town of Tarentum. Antony would send 130 ships to help Octavius against Sextus Pompeius, a son of Pompey who ruled the island of Sicily, just south of Rome. In return, Octavius agreed to send twenty thousand soldiers to join Antony's campaigns in the East. After the Treaty of Tarentum, Octavius asked Rome's ablest general, Marcus Agrippa, to lead the campaign against Sextus Pompeius.

Despite the treaty, many people in Rome saw that the Roman world was not big enough for Antony and Octavius. Each meeting between the two men started rumors of another civil war. Growing uneasy and

A modern reconstruction of the ancient Roman Forum, a section of Rome that served as the center of government

suspicious of Octavius in Rome, Antony and Octavia left for Antony's domains in the East. On the Greek island of Corfu, Octavia grew ill and Antony sent her back to Rome. She was pregnant with Antony's child and could not join him in any military campaigns. Many Romans falsely assumed that she was leaving because Antony had rejected her. To them, Antony's action represented a rebuke to Octavia and a personal insult to her brother.

Antony continued to Antioch, a city in Syria. Though he had not seen Cleopatra in years, it was she he wanted by his side. He sent her a message asking her to join him. Cleopatra had long awaited this moment and almost immediately left Alexandria for Antioch. There, the two may have conducted a marriage ceremony. The ceremony would have shocked many Romans, since Roman law prohibited marriage to more than one person. Antony and Cleopatra began appearing together on coins in Asia Minor and Egypt.

Always politically minded, the reunited lovers struck a bargain. Cleopatra agreed to build a fleet of ships for Antony and would keep her promise to support Antony's campaign in Parthia with money and soldiers. (Cleopatra's help became even more valuable to Antony because Octavius never sent the twenty thousand soldiers he had promised Antony—perhaps as a rebuke for sending Octavia back to Rome.) In return, Antony agreed to turn over most of his eastern territories—including Asia Minor, the island of Cyprus,

A silver coin portrait of Mark Antony, left, *and Cleopatra,* right, *from 32* B.C.

Phoenicia (modern Lebanon), and Jordan—to her. He refused, however, to turn over Judaea. Even though Cleopatra desperately wanted the land, Antony saw Herod, Judaea's king, as a useful ally in the Middle East.

With this grant of land, Antony made Cleopatra the queen of one of the largest Egyptian realms in history. Her rule was extended to include many wealthy cities of the Middle East. The valuable forests of Asia Minor and Phoenicia also came under Egyptian control and would supply the timber necessary for a huge Egyptian fleet of warships. (Antony would need these warships to replace the ships he had turned over to Octavius months earlier.)

Antony's "gifts" helped his alliance with Cleopatra but caused a scandal in Rome. To the Romans, Antony had no right to give away what was not his. He had given Roman territories, ruled by Roman governors, to the hated foreigner Cleopatra. Octavius and his friends did nothing to calm the outrage many Romans felt over these acts.

ANTONY'S CAMPAIGN

After several years of planning, Antony was finally prepared to march into Parthia. He was confident that his army could succeed where Crassus had failed. Antony had the support of Cleopatra as well as the Armenian king, Artavasdes, who pledged to reinforce Antony in the campaign.

In the spring of 36 B.C., the Romans began their mission. Antony crossed into Armenia, a kingdom lying just north of Parthia. From there he planned to invade Parthia. He divided his forces in two—a main army and a baggage train with a small guard. The baggage train contained Antony's siege equipment, which was needed to defeat the walled Parthian cities. But when the main army forged ahead, the slower-moving baggage train was suddenly attacked and destroyed. The Armenian king had turned against Antony, allowing the Parthians to ambush the Romans. Thousands of Roman soldiers lost their lives. Many others deserted.

Antony was forced to halt his infantry before he ever entered Parthia. Without siege equipment, such as catapults, battering rams, and towers for attacking high city walls, he could do nothing. Worse, winter was coming, and his army was running out of food. In October, 36 B.C., Antony turned back through Armenia to Syria. During the retreat, hit-and-run attacks as well as disease and hunger killed more than twenty thousand Roman soldiers. By the time Antony's once-proud army reached Syria, nearly half of the troops that had started out the previous spring were dead.

Antony had wanted to march on Parthia to bring glory to himself and his army. But the campaign designed to make him the equal of Alexander and Caesar had ended in complete failure.

One of the most famous structures of the ancient world was the Pharos (lighthouse) of Alexandria.

Chapter **SIX**

RULERS OF THE EAST

As **ANTONY RETURNED TO ANTIOCH IN SYRIA,** messengers brought news of the failed campaign to Egypt and Rome. Antony soon sent for Cleopatra, who had just given birth to his son Ptolemy Philadelphus.

In January of 35 B.C., Cleopatra arrived in Antioch, bringing winter clothing and money for Antony's soldiers. Later that year, Antony and Cleopatra returned together to Alexandria. Antony began preparing for another military campaign, this time against the Armenian king, that would avenge his humiliation in Parthia.

Octavia heard of the disastrous campaign. At her brother's urging, she set out from Rome in March, taking ships and troops that he supplied. (Instead of sending all of the ships Octavius had promised

Antony at Brundisium, however, Octavius sent only a few ships—an intentional insult to Antony.) Octavia had another important mission: she wanted to bring Antony back to the capital and reconcile him with her brother. But before she could reach Egypt, Antony sent her a message. She was to send the ships forward, but she herself was to turn back to Rome. Antony had decided to remain in the East with Cleopatra.

Antony may have made this decision out of fear of Octavius's growing power in Rome. Octavius had recently defeated Sextus Pompeius in Sicily. Then, after a disagreement with Lepidus, Octavius had dismissed him from the Triumvirate, bringing the troubled "group of three" to an official end. If Octavius was strong enough and confident enough to simply get rid of Lepidus in this way, what would he do if Antony returned?

Antony knew that he could trust Cleopatra. She had shown herself completely loyal to him. She also ruled a wealthy and peaceful country that could provide him with limitless money, soldiers, and glory. Rather than live among the dangerous civil wars and intrigues of Rome, where Octavius ruled, Antony could live as a pharaoh—as the New Dionysus—in Cleopatra's country.

Antony and Cleopatra began another round of festivities and merrymaking. Cleopatra wanted Antony in Alexandria and lavished as much attention and glory upon him as she could. Together, they posed as deities in religious ceremonies and led processions through the Alexandrian streets. They formed a society of friends they called the Order of the Inimitable Livers. Their circle turned her palace into a great stage for endless music, dancing, feasting, and pleasure.

THE DONATIONS OF ALEXANDRIA

Still determined to achieve a glorious military victory, Antony marched to Armenia and captured Artavasdes in 34 B.C. Antony brought the king back to Alexandria and displayed him as a prisoner in a grand celebration, in which Antony held public banquets and distributed money and gifts as part of the festivities. During the processions, the god-rulers Antony and Cleopatra glamorously displayed themselves as Dionysus and Isis. According to a Roman writer, Velleius Paterculus, Antony "had given orders that he should be called the [Dionysus], and indeed in a procession at Alexandria he had personified [Dionysus], his head bound with an ivy wreath, his person enveloped in the saffron robe of gold, holding in his hand the sacred wand, wearing the buckskins, and riding in the Bacchic chariot." Though Antony allegedly did not intend the festivities to be a Roman triumph (it was prohibited to hold triumphs outside Rome), the Romans were outraged.

A few days after this event, Antony and Cleopatra held another spectacular public ceremony. Seated on golden thrones, they named Cleopatra queen of Egypt, Cyprus, and the southern part of Syria. They also

This ancient Greek vase painting shows the god Dionysus, with whom Antony identified himself. By Antony's time, the worship of Dionysus was commonplace in the East.

proclaimed their children as the new heirs to the Roman provinces of the East. Their son Ptolemy Philadelphus would rule northern Syria and several small kingdoms in Asia Minor. Alexander Helios was granted Armenia, Media, and Parthia (which Antony had not yet conquered). Cleopatra Selene was granted Cyrene (the eastern part of modern-day Libya) and the island of Crete. Antony also declared that Caesarion, the son of Cleopatra and Julius Caesar, had become Caesar's heir and would some day rule in the West. Antony and Cleopatra obviously intended to wrest this territory from Octavius's grasp.

The ceremony came to be known as the Donations

of Alexandria. It was Antony's way of paying back Cleopatra for her allegiance and support, and it was Cleopatra's way of claiming the Roman Antony as her coruler. Cleopatra had maneuvered herself and her children onto the thrones of a Ptolemaic empire much larger than any territory ever ruled by the pharaohs of Egypt. But the Donations of Alexandria would prove effective only if she and Antony could succeed in conquering and holding these lands.

PROPAGANDA

To Cleopatra, the Donations of Alexandria symbolized the beginning of a new dynasty in Alexandria. For the Romans, it symbolized something entirely different. If it succeeded, the dynasty founded by Antony and Cleopatra would mean an end to the Roman government and Roman mastery over the Mediterranean world.

Octavius knew how to turn these events to his advantage. He immediately started a propaganda campaign against Antony and Cleopatra. Octavius announced that Antony was a traitor to Rome, ruling only for himself and not on behalf of the Roman people. The cause of his treachery was plain for all to see: Antony had been blinded by love for the corrupt and greedy Cleopatra, who wanted to make Alexandria the new Rome.

Octavius declared that under Cleopatra's evil influence, Antony had ignored tradition and held a triumph in Alexandria, instead of in Rome. In the

Donations of Alexandria, he had even given away Roman territories, which, according to Roman law, only Roman governors appointed by the Senate could rule. Octavius proclaimed:

> Who would not tear his hair at the sight of Roman soldiers serving as bodyguards of the queen? Who would not weep when he sees and hears what Antony has become? He has abandoned his whole ancestral way of life, has embraced alien and barbaric customs. And to crown it all, he bestows gifts of whole islands and parts of continents as though he were master of the entire earth and sea.

Octavius then revealed what he claimed was Mark Antony's will to the people of Rome. In it, Antony had allegedly written that he wished to be buried in Egypt—a dire insult to Rome. Antony had also declared his children by Cleopatra (an Egyptian), rather than those he had had by Octavia (a Roman), to be his heirs. Whether this was actually in Antony's will or not, Octavius succeeded in making his point. Though some Romans were still loyal to Antony, many became convinced that he had become an enemy of Rome.

Antony had grievances against Octavius, too—though Antony was not in Rome to gather sympathy from Roman listeners. Octavius had promised to send twenty thousand troops to help Antony campaign in the Middle East and Parthia but had sent only two

Octavius, shown here, *convinced the Romans that Antony was under Cleopatra's evil influence and that the lovers should both be defeated by force of arms.*

thousand. Octavius had dismissed Lepidus from the Triumvirate without consulting Antony. Octavius had not returned the ships he borrowed from Antony for the conquest of Sicily. And Octavius had awarded land in Rome only to soldiers loyal to him and none to Antony's soldiers. To return insults, Antony officially divorced the loyal Octavia, who had tried to end the rivalry between the two men.

This battle of personalities ruptured the ties of marriage and power sharing that had once united Antony and Octavius. As the people of Rome and Egypt could plainly see, Antony had made his choice: he would stay with Cleopatra in Egypt. He was no longer welcome in Rome.

It was becoming very obvious to Octavius and Antony that, sooner or later, the two men would be fighting with armies. They began gathering their forces in preparation for the unavoidable battle.

CONFLICT

Slowly, Antony moved his forces toward Rome for the showdown. In 33 B.C., Antony and Cleopatra settled in Ephesus, in Asia Minor. There they assembled a fleet of more than five hundred ships that had been built in Alexandria. Skilled Greek crews that Antony had hired would row and sail the ships. An army of fifty thousand Romans and eighty thousand Eastern troops gathered in Asia Minor to serve under Antony's command. Early in the next year, nearly three hundred of the nine hundred Roman senators left Rome to show their support for Antony. With his larger army and greater skill as a general, Antony appeared to be the probable winner in the coming battle—and the senators wanted to be on his side.

Confident of a victory against Octavius, Antony and Cleopatra traveled slowly across Greece and toward Rome. They stopped at the island of Samos "and there they made merry":

> While nearly the whole world was filled with groans and lamentations this one island for many

days resounded with the music of flutes and harps. The theaters were filled, and choruses competed against one another. Every city sent an ox for sacrifice and kings vied with one another in entertainments and gifts. Everywhere men began to ask how on earth the conquerors would celebrate their victory when their festivities at the opening of the war were so expensive.

From Samos, Antony and Cleopatra sailed across the Aegean Sea to Athens, Greece. Antony knew that he could defeat Octavius in a land battle, as his army was much larger. What Antony didn't yet realize, however, was that Marcus Agrippa (Octavius's top commander) was planning to outmaneuver him at sea.

Antony decided not to continue across the Adriatic Sea to Rome. He knew that if Cleopatra stayed with him, it would look like an attack on Rome. To many Romans, Cleopatra posed a dire threat. If she and Antony defeated Octavius, she would become queen of Rome as well as Egypt. Many of the Roman senators and generals at Antony's side told him that Cleopatra was making him unpopular. It might be best, some hinted, if Cleopatra returned to Egypt and allowed Antony to face his rival alone. Others whispered something much more sinister to Antony: he should have the queen murdered and then lay claim to Egypt himself.

Cleopatra steadfastly refused to leave Antony's side. Earlier, in Alexandria, she had ordered servants to store her immense treasury of gold and jewelry aboard her royal flagship. Cleopatra's treasury would help Antony pay and supply his troops and defeat Octavius, and she was determined to share the victory. If she returned to Egypt, she announced, her navy and her treasury would go with her.

Antony resolved to keep Cleopatra at his side. He would wait for Octavius in Greece, where Caesar and Pompey had fought Brutus and Cassius. A final battle on this neutral ground would decide the future of Rome and Egypt.

In Rome, Octavius prepared for the battle by declaring war in 32 B.C.—not on Antony, but on the foreigner Cleopatra. Octavius believed this action would bring more Romans—who didn't want another civil war

Portrait of Marcus Agrippa, Octavius's top military commander

between Roman leaders and who believed Cleopatra was a bad influence—to his side. Octavius arranged for the Senate to dismiss Antony as a triumvir. To further rile up the Romans against Antony, Octavius led a riotous procession to the Temple of Bellona, a temple dedicated to the Roman goddess of war. Following tradition, he threw a bloodstained spear toward the east, in the direction of the enemy, as the Romans loudly cheered. Octavius's army then marched south to the ports of Brundisium and Tarentum. The troops camped for the winter, while Octavius's commanders readied the battleships and their crews for the coming spring.

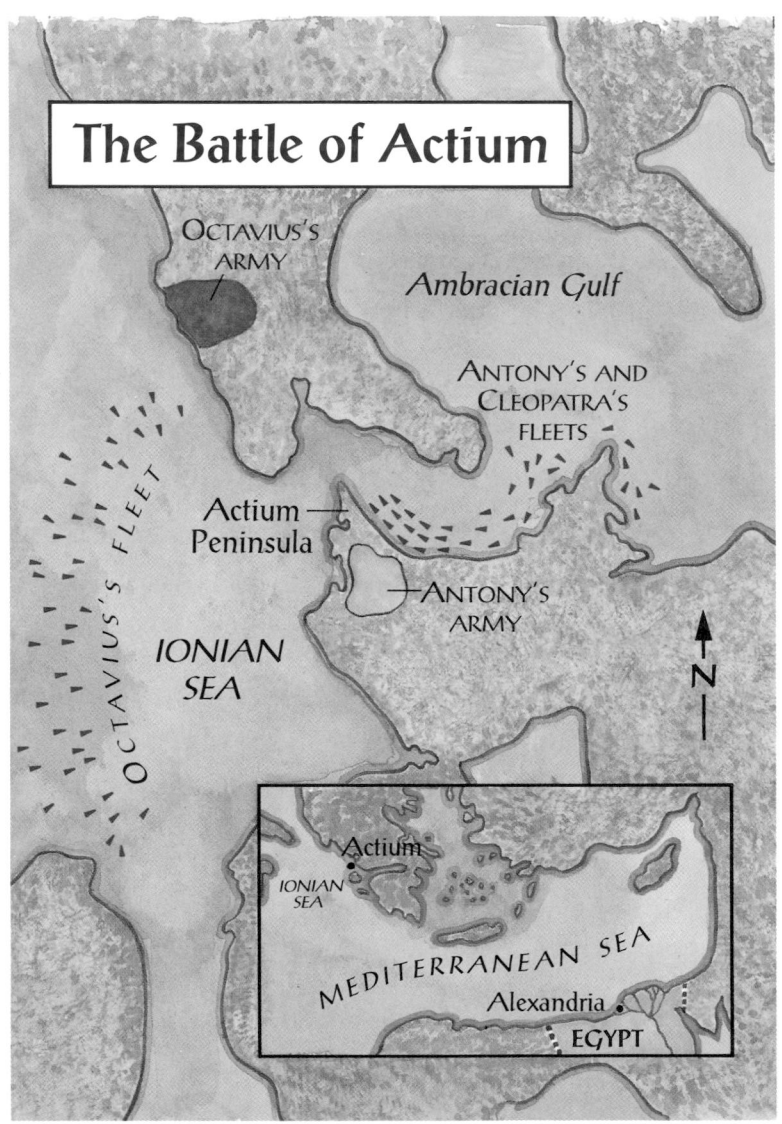

The Battle of Actium

OCTAVIUS'S ARMY

Ambracian Gulf

ANTONY'S AND CLEOPATRA'S FLEETS

OCTAVIUS'S FLEET

Actium Peninsula

ANTONY'S ARMY

IONIAN SEA

N

Actium

IONIAN SEA

MEDITERRANEAN SEA

Alexandria

EGYPT

Cleopatra and Antony faced off with Octavius in 31 B.C.

Chapter **SEVEN**

THE BATTLE OF ACTIUM

IN THE FALL OF **32** B.C., CLEOPATRA AND ANTONY moved their forces to western Greece, just across the Ionian Sea from Italy. They split up their navy and sent the fleets to patrol the long, rugged Ionian seacoast. The bulk of their ships were positioned in a well-protected gulf, the Ambracian Gulf, behind a point called Actium. A smaller fleet stayed near the island of Corfu, and another fleet was stationed at the southwestern tip of Greece. Antony placed troops along the southern shore of the gulf, a marshy and mosquito-infested arm of the Ionian Sea.

Octavius had appointed Marcus Agrippa to lead the campaign against Antony and Cleopatra. Learning of the divided forces of the enemy, Agrippa decided to attack them piece by piece. In March of 31 B.C., he attacked and defeated Antony and Cleopatra's fleet at the southwestern tip of Greece. Using this area as headquarters, Agrippa cut off Antony and Cleopatra from any supplies and reinforcements from Egypt. To keep from starving, Antony's soldiers had to forage in the barren mountain valleys near the gulf.

Following Agrippa's first victory against Antony and Cleopatra, Octavius landed his army at Epirus, on the Greek mainland north of the gulf. Octavius led his troops south and camped on a peninsula jutting into the gulf from the north. Deciding he would fight Octavius at this point, Antony brought his troops to a peninsula on the southern side of the gulf. The two armies faced each other across a narrow channel at Actium.

LAYING THE TRAP

Agrippa's navy captured Antony and Cleopatra's second fleet near Corfu. Agrippa then sailed to Actium, where he placed his fleet just outside the gulf. Here he could prevent Antony's troops and the Egyptian navy from escaping.

On the mainland, Octavius patiently waited. He knew that Antony's troops still might defeat him in a land battle. So he ordered his troops to remain on the narrow peninsula to the north of Actium, where Antony wouldn't be able to assemble a force large enough to defeat them.

Antony and Cleopatra, meanwhile, found themselves

trapped at Actium. With Agrippa's ships cutting off reinforcements from Egypt, their supplies were running low. Their soldiers began to go hungry; many died of malaria and other diseases. Instead of attacking Octavius, Antony argued with Cleopatra and his generals on a strategy for escape.

Cleopatra thought Antony should board his soldiers on the Egyptian fleet and attack Agrippa's ships. They would fight Agrippa's navy, destroy as many of his ships as possible, and then sail immediately for the Italian Peninsula. There, Antony's soldiers would be able to stop Octavius from returning. Meanwhile, Antony could gather a new army and march on Rome to claim the victory.

Canidius Crassus, Antony's second in command, had a much different plan. He advised Antony to retreat immediately from Actium. Roman soldiers fought on land, Crassus said, not at sea. Antony should fight Octavius somewhere else in Greece. The best place would be Macedonia, a region of open plains where Antony's army would be able to defeat Octavius in a large land battle. But this strategy would mean abandoning the Egyptian fleet to fight Agrippa alone. If this happened, Antony and Cleopatra knew, Agrippa would probably destroy the Egyptian fleet.

Cleopatra was determined not to see her fleet left behind. She felt certain that her powerful fleet could defeat the lighter Roman ships. She would destroy Agrippa and have Octavius and his army at her mercy. Going against the wishes of his generals, Antony took

Cleopatra's side. He would stay with the queen and fight it out at Actium.

The summer of 31 B.C. wore on. Heat and illness affected troops on both sides. Antony's troops grew hungry and desperate. Many of them deserted Antony to join Octavius. Antony and Cleopatra quarreled violently with their generals and with each other.

In late August, Antony decided on his plan. Instead of trying for victory, which by this point seemed impossible, he would escape with as many ships as he could. He ordered twenty-two thousand soldiers to prepare to attack Agrippa's fleet and then slip past them to the open sea and freedom. Antony and Cleopatra's crews stored their sails in readiness for the getaway after the fight.

Antony instructed Crassus to lead the land troops in a retreat to the east after the battle and make their way to Asia Minor. Antony said he would later join them and retreat to Egypt. If Antony and Cleopatra could hold their forces together, they would be able to stop any attack Octavius might later make on Egypt.

On the second of September, Antony and Cleopatra moved toward Agrippa's ships. The two fleets slowly engaged. Using slings, Antony's men rained down heavy stones on the Roman ships. They threw long javelins toward the enemy across the water. Ships on both sides used their battering rams to tear holes in the enemy hulls. Whenever two ships approached, grappling hooks were sent out to pull the enemy alongside. Soldiers

A woodcut showing the battle at Actium

leaped across the rails and decks and fought hand to hand with swords, daggers, and spears.

Agrippa's ships were smaller but easier to turn. This allowed them to avoid the larger Egyptian ships while maneuvering to ram them over and over again. A historian named Cassius Dio wrote, "Octavius's ships resembled cavalry, now launching a charge, and now retreating, since they could attack or draw off as they chose, while Antony's were like heavy infantry, warding off the enemy's efforts to ram them."

The long lines of opposing ships scattered, and the battle turned into a free-for-all. Meanwhile, Cleopatra held back her own squadron of sixty ships and watched from her flagship. Antony drew Agrippa and his ships slowly to the north, away from Cleopatra's squadron, which slowly rowed away to the west. Suddenly, Cleopatra's ships raised their sails and headed south, riding the wind into the open sea. Shocking everybody except perhaps Cleopatra, Antony followed his lover. In the book *Roman History,* Cassius Dio describes the end of the battle:

> Cleopatra, riding at anchor behind the combatants ... was tortured by the agony of the long suspense and by the constant and fearful expectation of either possible outcome, and so she suddenly turned to flight herself and raised the signal for her own subjects. ... Antony thought they were fleeing, not at the bidding of Cleopatra, but through fear because they felt themselves vanquished, and so he followed them.

Many historians believe that Antony expected to lose the battle and wanted Cleopatra to escape this way. The lovers certainly knew that in this part of Greece, a strong northwest wind often rises in the late afternoon and blows directly toward Egypt. While Antony followed Cleopatra, the rest of his navy fought on into the night. By morning, Antony's ships had either sunk or retreated back toward the gulf. The next day, the survivors surrendered to Octavius.

ESCAPE TO EGYPT

Antony and Cleopatra sailed to Egypt with Cleopatra's huge royal treasury—the money that would allow them to raise another army and fight again another day. Antony was a broken man, however. He had lost a battle and, even worse, deserted his men.

Antony's head general, Crassus, brought the rest of Antony's army away from the gulf. Octavius's army soon caught up with Crassus. Instead of attacking, Octavius announced an amnesty. He would reward enemy soldiers with land if they would abandon Antony's cause. The army quickly accepted the offer. The loyal Crassus himself escaped to Alexandria to give Antony the news.

Octavius, however, could not press on immediately to Egypt. Many of his soldiers were expecting a reward in money and land for their victory. And violent rebellions were breaking out in Rome, where the people had paid taxes to help Octavius raise his army. Octavius hurried back to calm the situation, giving Antony and Cleopatra time to gather new forces in Egypt.

Octavius knew that he couldn't raise any more money by taxing his territories in the West, including Rome. The only way to pay his soldiers was to conquer Egypt, defeat Antony and Cleopatra, and capture Cleopatra's treasury.

Octavius also knew that Antony would soon begin raising a new army with Cleopatra's help. Octavius waited until the spring of 30 B.C., when the dangerous winter storms in the Mediterranean Sea had passed. Then he left Rome, this time for Alexandria, where he would force another, hopefully final, battle with Antony and Cleopatra.

Cleopatra, in traditional Egyptian stone relief, from the Temple of Hathor, in Dendera, Egypt

Chapter **EIGHT**

THE POISON SNAKE

AS THE NEWS OF THE BATTLE OF ACTIUM SPREAD, rulers who had been allies of Cleopatra and Antony switched their loyalty. The leaders of kingdoms in Greece, Asia Minor, and North Africa, and even Herod of Judaea (who owed his crown to Antony), swore an oath to help Octavius, the leader they saw as victor. They realized that if they supported Octavius before the victory was complete, they would be rewarded when Antony and Cleopatra were defeated. Cleopatra's enemies volunteered to help Octavius by attacking Egypt from the east and west.

Antony and Cleopatra could do nothing but wait for Octavius and his forces to arrive. Believing his situation was hopeless, Antony asked Octavius for mercy and for the chance to live in Alexandria as a private citizen, stripped of all rank and privilege. Octavius refused. Depressed and broken, Antony built a small house, which he called the Timoneum, near the Pharos lighthouse. There he lived alone, staying apart from Cleopatra and from his officers.

Cleopatra had been in many difficult situations before. She sent messengers and gifts to Octavius, asking that he allow her to live, and also allow Egypt to remain independent. She also asked that Caesarion be allowed to inherit the throne of Egypt. To place Caesarion out of harm's way, she sent him away from Alexandria into the desert near the Red Sea, where she believed he would be safe.

Cleopatra was determined to fight until she could fight no more—and then to flee. She ordered the remaining Egyptian ships to be hauled ashore and dragged across land to the Gulf of Suez. There she planned to launch them into the Red Sea and escape to India.

THE LAST DAYS OF CLEOPATRA

Octavius accepted Cleopatra's gifts but refused all of her pleas. He had no intention of allowing Egypt its independence or of allowing Caesarion to become its ruler. Once Octavius left Rome in the spring of 30 B.C., he marched into Asia Minor and prepared for an attack on Egypt. He arrived in Egypt that summer.

Knowing his defeat was almost certain, Antony pulled himself together. He moved back to the palace,

where he and Cleopatra again held festivities, ceremonies, and lavish feasts. Cleopatra and Antony re-
named their circle of friends the Order of the
Inseparable in Death. They swore to entertain themselves until they would either escape or meet their
deaths together at Octavius's hands.

In a final attempt to save his Eastern empire, Antony
marched a small army out of the city to meet the
Romans. He attacked Octavius's cavalry (soldiers on
horseback), at first driving them back. But Octavius's
forces quickly regrouped and forced Antony's army to
retreat. Antony sent a messenger to Octavius, challeng-
ing the younger man to a hand-to-hand combat to settle their differences. Octavius refused.

Antony then attempted to bribe the enemy soldiers
to come over to his side. None accepted. The next day,
the Egyptian navy in Alexandria surrendered to
Octavius without a fight. Antony's cavalry soldiers also
laid down their arms, while his foot soldiers fled
into Alexandria.

In the meantime, an army of Arabians marched
toward the Gulf of Suez, where Cleopatra's ships lay
at anchor. The Arabians did not want Cleopatra to escape and then prepare an attack on them. They
burned the entire Egyptian fleet, leaving Cleopatra no
chance to escape.

The Roman army moved into Alexandria and surrounded the royal palace. Cleopatra and three of her
servants fled the palace and locked themselves inside

a vast mausoleum. Cleopatra had prepared this temple to hold her own tomb. Here she planned to die, and here she would be buried. She ordered her servants to carry her royal treasury into the mausoleum and hide it in a storeroom.

Antony received a false message that Cleopatra was already dead. On hearing the news, Antony turned to his faithful servant Eros and asked the man to kill him. Unable to commit the deed, Eros turned his sword on himself instead and died at Antony's feet. Antony pulled another sword from its scabbard and thrust it into his stomach. He dropped the weapon and staggered to the ground.

The news of Antony's impending death spread quickly. Upon Cleopatra's orders, two servants soon arrived outside the mausoleum with Antony lying on a stretcher. Though Antony was dying, Cleopatra would not unlock the doors, for fear that the Roman soldiers patrolling the streets would rush inside and seize her. She ordered her servants to sneak Antony in from one of the high windows. Using ropes, the servants gently lowered Antony's stretcher to the floor. When she saw Antony, Cleopatra began to sob with grief. Antony uttered his final words to her, asking her not to pity him. He had "fallen not ignobly, a Roman by a Roman overcome." He gasped for his last breath and died.

Octavius entered Alexandria that day. Upon hearing of Antony's death, he immediately sent his aide, Proculeius, to the mausoleum. Proculeius led a small company of guards through the mausoleum window, where Antony had been smuggled in just hours earlier, and captured the queen.

Octavius allowed Cleopatra to attend Antony's funeral. Afterward, Octavius announced that he would take Cleopatra back to Rome as a prisoner and parade her in his coming triumph, just as Caesar had done to Arsinoë. Octavius may not have really intended to do this, since the Romans had objected so strongly to the same treatment of Arsinoë. He probably intended to scare Cleopatra into committing suicide. He asked his guards to leave Cleopatra and her two attendants alone, believing the queen would take her own life rather than suffer further humiliation.

Octavius was right. Cleopatra bathed, dressed beautifully as Isis, and ate a sumptuous last meal before carrying out a dramatic suicide.

No one knows exactly how Cleopatra died. Legend says that Cleopatra ordered her servants to hide an Egyptian asp (a poisonous snake) in a basket of figs. The servants brought the basket past the guards standing outside Cleopatra's room. Cleopatra took the snake from the basket and held it before her. In Shakespeare's *Antony and Cleopatra,* Cleopatra says:

> With thy sharp teeth this knot intricate
> Of life at once untie: poor venomous fool,
> Be angry, and dispatch. O couldst thou speak,
> That I might hear thee call great Octavius ass.

The snake struck Cleopatra, and the poison quickly did its work. Her servants also committed suicide. Egypt's Ptolemaic dynasty and the reign of thirty-nine-year-old Cleopatra had come to an end.

THIS KNOT UNTIED

It is uncertain whether the sixteen-year-old Caesarion, hoping to escape Octavius and the Romans, actually made it out of Alexandria. By most accounts, he fled the city. After the death of his mother, Caesarion heard from his tutor, Rhodon, that Octavius might pardon him. He would not be allowed to rule over Egypt, as Cleopatra had hoped, but he might be allowed to live. Caesarion returned to Alexandria, where he discovered that he had been betrayed. Octavius would not allow such a dangerous rival to remain alive. Caesarion was captured and executed.

It is believed that the rest of Cleopatra's children were captured and made to walk in Octavius's triumph in Rome. Later, Cleopatra Selene escaped to the African province of Mauretania, where she married King Juba II. Alexander Helios and Ptolemy Philadelphus also fled and survived—where and how long, nobody knows.

THE ROMAN EMPIRE

Later in 30 B.C., Octavius made Egypt a Roman province. Cleopatra's treasury was brought back to Rome, allowing Octavius to buy land for the soldiers who had served at Actium. Octavius's victory officially

A nineteenth-century painting called The Death of Cleopatra

transformed Rome from a republic into an empire. Ironically, it became an absolute monarchy, in the tradition of Ptolemaic Egypt. Octavius ruled as the first emperor, with the title of Augustus Caesar in memory of his great uncle Julius Caesar.

The month of Octavius's final victory over Antony and Cleopatra was named Augustus in his honor, following July, the month named for Julius Caesar. Octavius built the city of Nicopolis (meaning Victory City in Greek) near Actium. He also initiated an athletic festival known as the Actiaca, to be held in Rome every four years, in celebration of his victory over Antony and Cleopatra.

Octavius would rule the Roman Empire until his death in 14 A.D. While Octavius (as Augustus) would go down in history as the founder of the Roman Empire, Antony and Cleopatra would be remembered in the West (much of whose ancient historical information has come from Rome) as unlucky lovers and as the defeated enemies of Rome.

Actress Elizabeth Taylor won fame and fortune for her portrayal of the Egyptian queen in the epic 1963 Hollywood film Cleopatra.

Chapter NINE

THE LEGENDS OF CLEOPATRA

FOR THE ROMANS, EVEN A DEAD CLEOPATRA represented a dangerous enemy and a treacherous woman. Roman historians loyal to Octavius and his successors criticized Cleopatra and belittled her life. They spread tales of Cleopatra's greed and immorality, ignoring her accomplishments as queen of Egypt. A typical account was written by the Roman historian Josephus, who declared:

> [T]here was no lawless deed which she did not commit; she had already caused the death by poisoning of her brother when he was only fifteen years old because she knew that he was to become king, and she had her sister Arsinoë killed. . . . In sum, nothing was enough by itself for

this extravagant woman, who was enslaved by her appetites, so that the whole world failed to satisfy the desires of her imagination.

Most chroniclers of Cleopatra's life, including Plutarch, lived long after the queen's death. Their information had been passed down through many generations. Much of it was distorted by Romans rewriting history to suit their own motives.

In fact, Cleopatra had a much greater effect on Rome than her enemies would admit. Octavius ruled the Roman Empire in much the same way that pharaohs had ruled Egypt for several millennia. The image of Augustus as a semidivine ruler surely took some inspiration from the Egyptians. Cleopatra's realm also became an important part of the Roman Empire, which depended on Egypt's grain and tribute. Cleopatra remained important to the city of Rome—her statue was still standing in the temple dedicated to Venus three hundred years after Caesar had raised it. Alexandrians and other Egyptians praised her memory, and a cult dedicated to her survived in the Mediterranean world for many years.

Much later, European painters saw Cleopatra and her dramatic story as an excellent subject for their works. A drawing by Michelangelo shows the head and shoulders of Cleopatra with a snake clinging to her body. Hundreds of other works show Cleopatra in the last minutes of her life, a snake in her hand,

Actors Vivien Leigh and Claude Rains starred in the 1946 film version of George Bernard Shaw's play Caesar and Cleopatra.

defeated but still beautiful. William Shakespeare's *Antony and Cleopatra* depicts Cleopatra as a clever and manipulative *femme fatale* (a beautiful woman who causes trouble and destruction). Antony is portrayed as a man who feels loyalty to his wife Octavia as well as a strong passion for Cleopatra—a love triangle that ends in his destruction.

In the twentieth century, Cleopatra became a favorite subject for playwrights and film directors. The Irish playwright George Bernard Shaw wrote a witty account of her relationship with Julius Caesar in his play *Caesar and Cleopatra*. The actress Theda Bara played Cleopatra as a "vamp" in a silent movie. Like a snake, the movie vamp could hypnotize men with her deep gaze. In 1962 Elizabeth Taylor played Cleopatra in another Hollywood film. Taylor's Cleopatra was an independent, energetic, and clever woman who had a

FINDING CLEOPATRA'S PALACE

n the year 335 A.D., a powerful earthquake struck Alexandria. Soon afterward, a tidal wave crashed into the city, flooding the shores of the eastern harbor and destroying many homes and monuments. Since that day, the palace district where Cleopatra lived has been lying under twenty feet of water, unseen and unexplored.

In June 1996, a French underwater explorer named Franck Goddio set out to find Cleopatra's drowned palace. With a team of sixteen experienced divers, he made 3,500 dives in the ancient eastern harbor. The team found paved streets, statues (one of them a sphinx and believed to be of Auletes), granite columns, and thousands of building fragments. They also found ancient piers and jetties.

Using an electronic measuring system, members of the expedition have been able to map the contours of streets and buildings from Cleopatra's time. Goddio's team carefully dragged a plumb bob, or weighted line, over the bottom of the harbor. As the bob rose and fell, the changing depths were charted, giving the contours of ancient streets, walls, and other ruins.

In the future, ancient Alexandria may be turned into an underwater archaeological park, where visitors can discover Cleopatra's palace by diving or by submarine. For the first time, historians and others can study the paths walked by Cleopatra, Antony, Caesar, and other figures of Alexandria's fascinating past.

taste for luxury and who had no problem matching wits with her enemies. Taylor made fifty thousand dollars a week for acting in the movie and, according to one writer, did all that she could to match Cleopatra's extravagance:

> In Rome she lived in a villa with fourteen rooms, or perhaps seventeen rooms, faced in pink marble. Every evening the cigarette holders, matchbooks, candles, flowers, and tablecloth were new, and matched her dress. She had full-length mirrors installed in her bathroom, where she bathed by candlelight. She brought three hundred dresses with her to Rome and threw away each one after one wearing.

In the form of plays, paintings, books, and movies, Cleopatra's memory lives on. More than two thousand years after her death, she continues to mystify and intrigue. Whether they believe Cleopatra was ruthless and immoral, or dedicated and brave, ancient and modern historians, artists, writers, directors, and others have agreed that this fascinating ancient queen proved herself the equal of any Ptolemaic king and of the Roman leaders she encountered. She has become a symbol of strength, intelligence, and ambition, recognized the world over.

THE LIFE OF CLEOPATRA VII

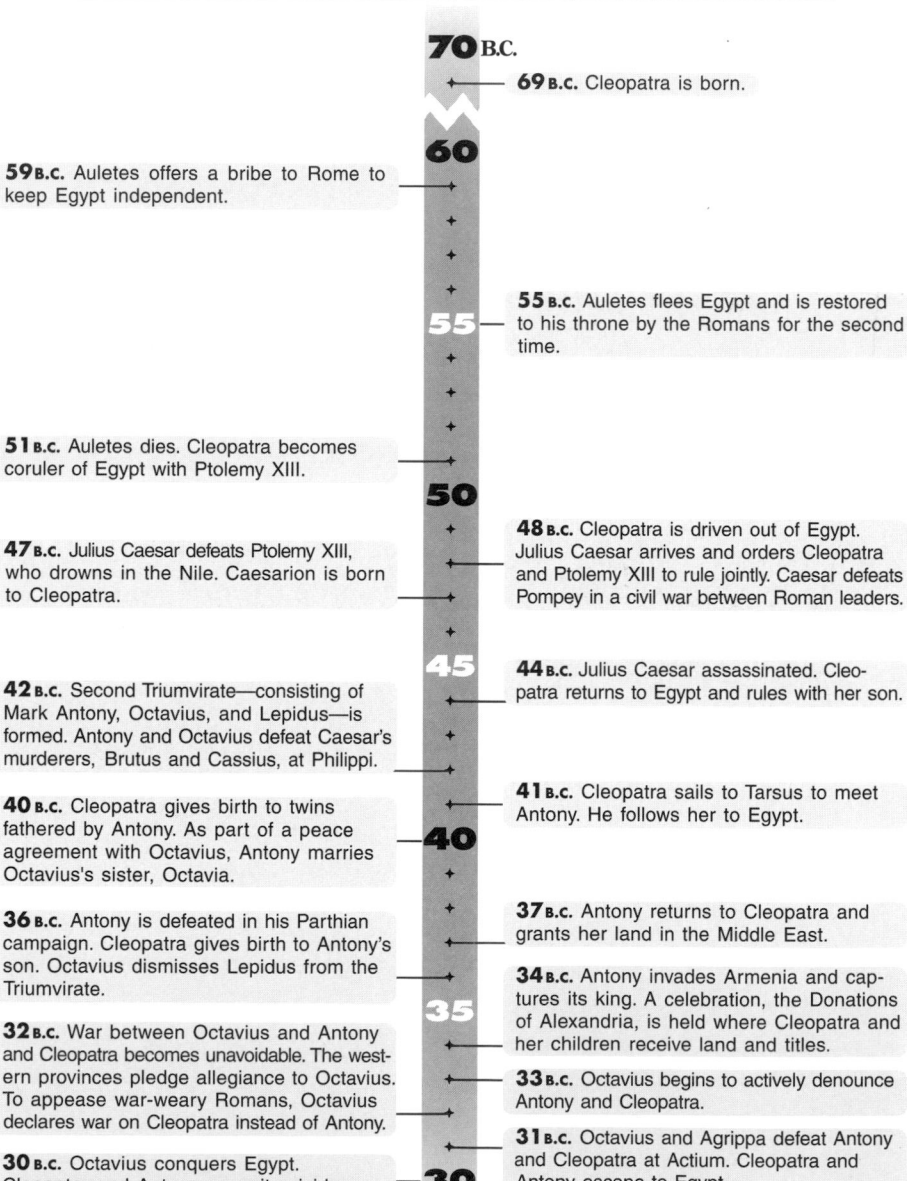

70 B.C.

69 B.C. Cleopatra is born.

60

59 B.C. Auletes offers a bribe to Rome to keep Egypt independent.

55 B.C. Auletes flees Egypt and is restored to his throne by the Romans for the second time.

55

51 B.C. Auletes dies. Cleopatra becomes coruler of Egypt with Ptolemy XIII.

50

48 B.C. Cleopatra is driven out of Egypt. Julius Caesar arrives and orders Cleopatra and Ptolemy XIII to rule jointly. Caesar defeats Pompey in a civil war between Roman leaders.

47 B.C. Julius Caesar defeats Ptolemy XIII, who drowns in the Nile. Caesarion is born to Cleopatra.

45

44 B.C. Julius Caesar assassinated. Cleopatra returns to Egypt and rules with her son.

42 B.C. Second Triumvirate—consisting of Mark Antony, Octavius, and Lepidus—is formed. Antony and Octavius defeat Caesar's murderers, Brutus and Cassius, at Philippi.

41 B.C. Cleopatra sails to Tarsus to meet Antony. He follows her to Egypt.

40 B.C. Cleopatra gives birth to twins fathered by Antony. As part of a peace agreement with Octavius, Antony marries Octavia's sister, Octavia.

40

37 B.C. Antony returns to Cleopatra and grants her land in the Middle East.

36 B.C. Antony is defeated in his Parthian campaign. Cleopatra gives birth to Antony's son. Octavius dismisses Lepidus from the Triumvirate.

34 B.C. Antony invades Armenia and captures its king. A celebration, the Donations of Alexandria, is held where Cleopatra and her children receive land and titles.

35

32 B.C. War between Octavius and Antony and Cleopatra becomes unavoidable. The western provinces pledge allegiance to Octavius. To appease war-weary Romans, Octavius declares war on Cleopatra instead of Antony.

33 B.C. Octavius begins to actively denounce Antony and Cleopatra.

31 B.C. Octavius and Agrippa defeat Antony and Cleopatra at Actium. Cleopatra and Antony escape to Egypt.

30 B.C. Octavius conquers Egypt. Cleopatra and Antony commit suicide.

30

SOURCES

1–2   Michael Grant, *Cleopatra: A Biography* (New York: Simon and Schuster, 1972), 115.

32   Plutarch, *Lives of the Noble Grecians and Romans* (New York: Random House, n.d.), 1119.

34   Michael Foss, *The Search for Cleopatra* (New York: Arcade, 1997), 71.

35   Plutarch, 864–865.

56   William Shakespeare, *The Works of William Shakespeare*, The Shakespeare Head Press Edition (New York: Oxford University Press, 1938), 598.

60–61   Plutarch, 1107.

63   Plutarch, 1119.

76   Grant, 161.

78   Don Nardo, *The Importance of Cleopatra* (San Diego, Calif.: Lucent Books, 1994), 68.

81   Ernle Bradford, *Cleopatra* (New York: Harcourt Brace Jovanovich, 1972), 215.

90   Cassius Dio, *Roman History*, vol. V (Cambridge, Mass.: Harvard University Press, 1917), 507–509.

96   Plutarch, 1148.

98   Shakespeare, 963.

101–102   Flavius Josephus, *Jewish Antiquities* (Cambridge, Mass.: Harvard University Press, 1955), 45.

105   Lucy Hughes-Hallett, *Cleopatra: Histories, Dreams and Distortions* (New York: Harper & Row, 1990), 289.

BIBLIOGRAPHY

Appian. *Appian's Roman History,* vol. IV. Cambridge, Mass.:
   Harvard University Press, 1955.

Bradford, Ernle. *Cleopatra.* New York: Harcourt Brace
   Jovanovich, 1972.

Brooks, Polly Schoyer. *Cleopatra: Goddess of Egypt, Enemy of
   Rome.* New York: Harper Collins, 1995.

Caesar, Julius. *Alexandrian, African, and Spanish Wars.*
   Cambridge: Harvard University Press, 1955.

Carcopino, Jerome. *Daily Life in Ancient Rome: The People and
   the City at the Height of the Empire.* New York: Bantam
   Books, 1971.

Dio, Cassius. *Roman History,* vol. V. Cambridge: Harvard
   University Press, 1917.

Foss, Michael. *The Search for Cleopatra.* New York: Arcade, 1997.

Grant, Michael. *Julius Caesar.* New York: M. Evans and Company,
   Inc., 1992.

_____ . *Cleopatra: A Biography.* New York: Simon and
   Schuster, 1972.

Hughes–Hallett, Lucy. *Cleopatra: Histories, Dreams and
   Distortions.* New York: Harper & Row, 1990.

Josephus, Flavius. *Jewish Antiquities.* Cambridge, Mass.: Harvard
   University Press, 1955.

Nardo, Don. *The Importance of Cleopatra.* San Diego, Calif.:
   Lucent Books, 1994.

Plutarch. *Lives of the Noble Grecians and Romans.* New York:
   Random House, n.d.

Rieland, Randy. "The Search for Cleopatra's Palace," *Discovery
   Channel Online,* n.d., <http://www.discovery.com/indep/
   newsfeatures/cleopatra/cleopatra> (n.d.).

Shakespeare, William. *The Works of William Shakespeare,* The
   Shakespeare Head Press Edition. New York: Oxford
   University Press, 1938.

INDEX

OTHER TITLES FROM LERNER AND A&E®:

ABOUT THE AUTHOR

Tom Streissguth lives in Florida and works as a writer and editor for book publishers all over the United States. He has written more than twenty-five nonfiction books for young people, including biographies and books on history, geography, and current events. His volumes in the BIOGRAPHY® series include *Legends of Dracula, Jesse Owens,* and *John Glenn.* Tom has also written scripts for television.

PHOTO ACKNOWLEDGMENTS

Art Resource, NY: (© Giraudon) p. 2, (© Scala) p. 15, (© Erich Lessing) pp. 19, 51, 76; E.T. Archive: (Louvre, Paris), p. 6, (Gallery of Modern Art, Rome) p. 52, (E.T. Archive) p. 92, (Fine Arts Museum, Bilbao) p. 99; North Wind Picture Archive, pp. 20, 89; University of Minnesota College of Architecture and Landscape Architecture, p. 23; The Granger Collection, New York, pp. 27, 30, 37, 40, 44, 64, 69, 79; The Bridgeman Art Library: (© Peter Willi/Louvre, Paris) p. 33, (The Stapleton Collection) p. 72; Mary Evans Picture Library: (© Douglas Dickins) p. 47, (© Alma Tadema in Century) p. 54; Archive Photos, pp. 57, 67, 82, 100; Photofest, p. 103

Front cover: Corbis
Back cover: Archive Photos
Maps by Laura Westlund, pp. 11, 84